Keep Counting
Cuenta, cuenta

Illustrated by **Ishan Zaidi**   Ilustraciones de **Ishan Zaidi**

TeachingStrategies™ • Washington D.C.

For Teaching Strategies, Inc.
Publisher: Larry Bram
Editorial Director: Hilary Parrish Nelson
VP Curriculum and Assessment: Cate Heroman
Product Manager: Kai-leé Berke
Book Development Team: Sherrie Rudick and Jan Greenberg
Project Manager: Jo A. Wilson

For Q2AMedia
Editorial Director: Bonnie Dobkin
Editor and Curriculum Adviser: Suzanne Barchers
Program Manager: Gayatri Singh
Creative Director: Simmi Sikka
Project Manager: Santosh Vasudevan
Illustrator: Ishan Zaidi
Designer: Ritu Chopra

Teaching Strategies, Inc.
P.O. Box 42243
Washington, DC 20015
www.TeachingStrategies.com

ISBN: 978-1-60617-145-5

Library of Congress Cataloging-in-Publication Data
Zaidi, Ishan.
  Keep counting / illustrated by Ishan Zaidi = Cuenta, cuenta / ilustraciones de Ishan Zaidi.
  cm.
  ISBN 978-1-60617-145-5
  1. Counting—Juvenile literature. I. Title. II. Title: Cuenta, cuenta.
  QA113.Z35 2010
  513.2'11—dc22
                          2010004465

CPSIA tracking label information:
RR Donnelley, Shenzhen, China
Date of Production: June 2014
Cohort: Batch 3

Printed and bound in China

7 8 9 10	15 14
Printing	Year Printed

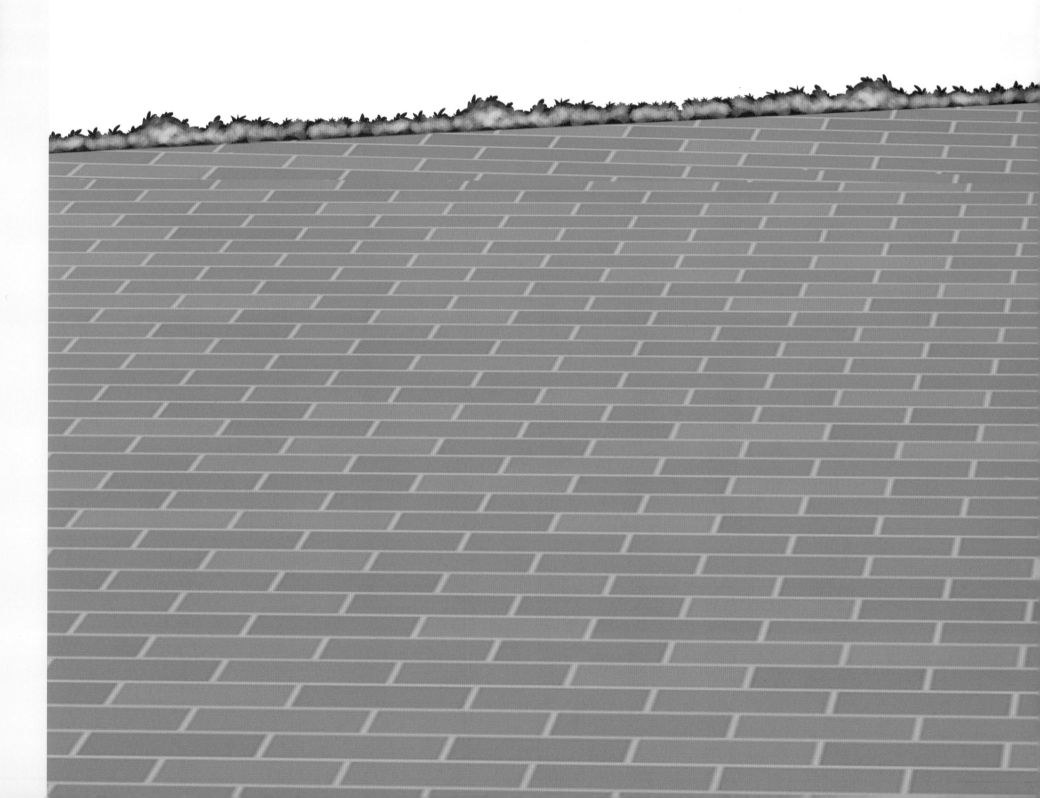

0

1

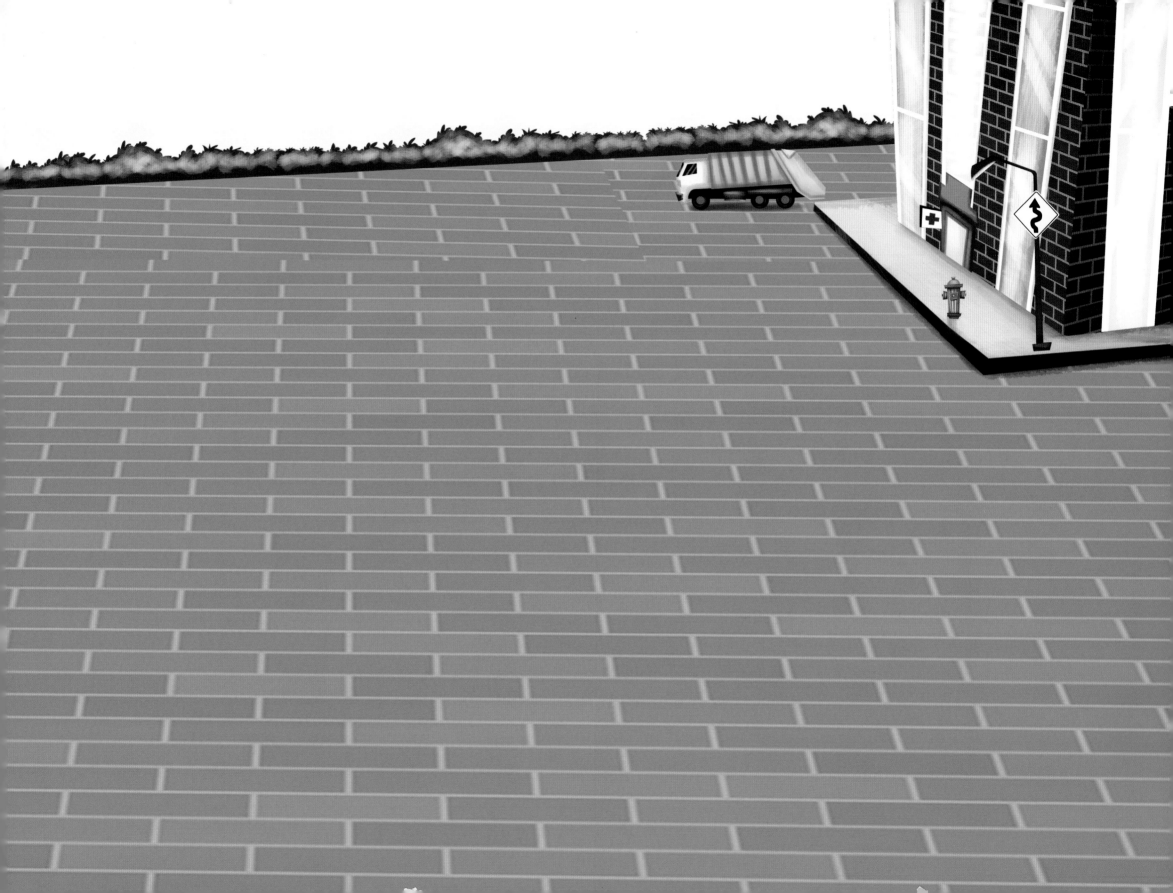

2

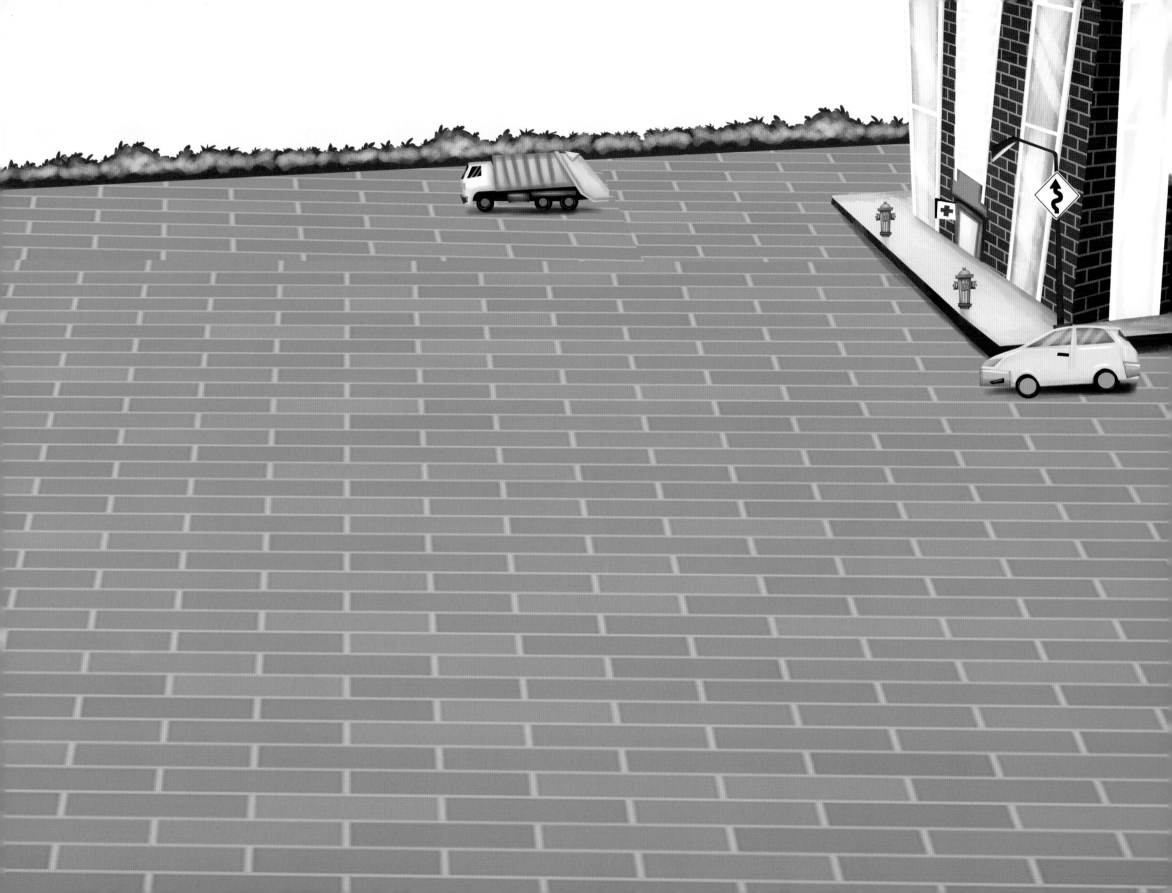

3

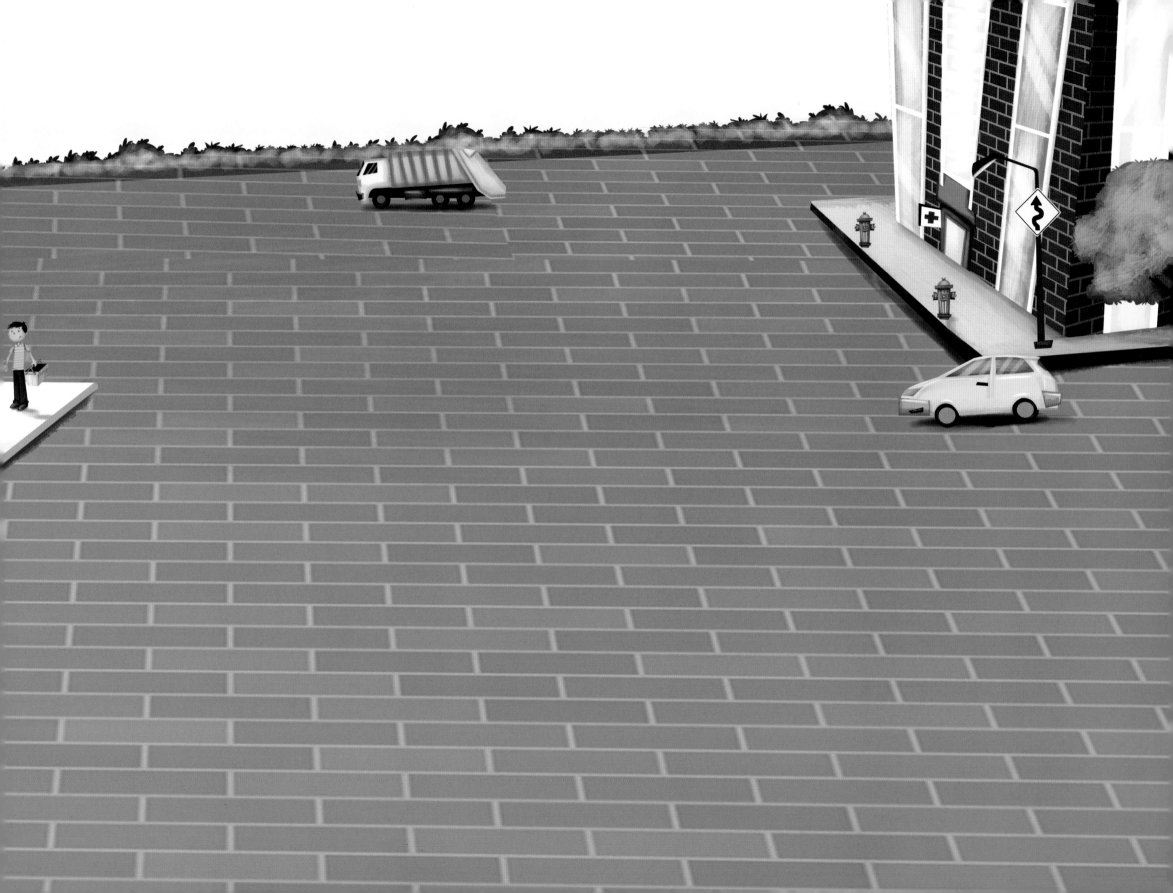

4

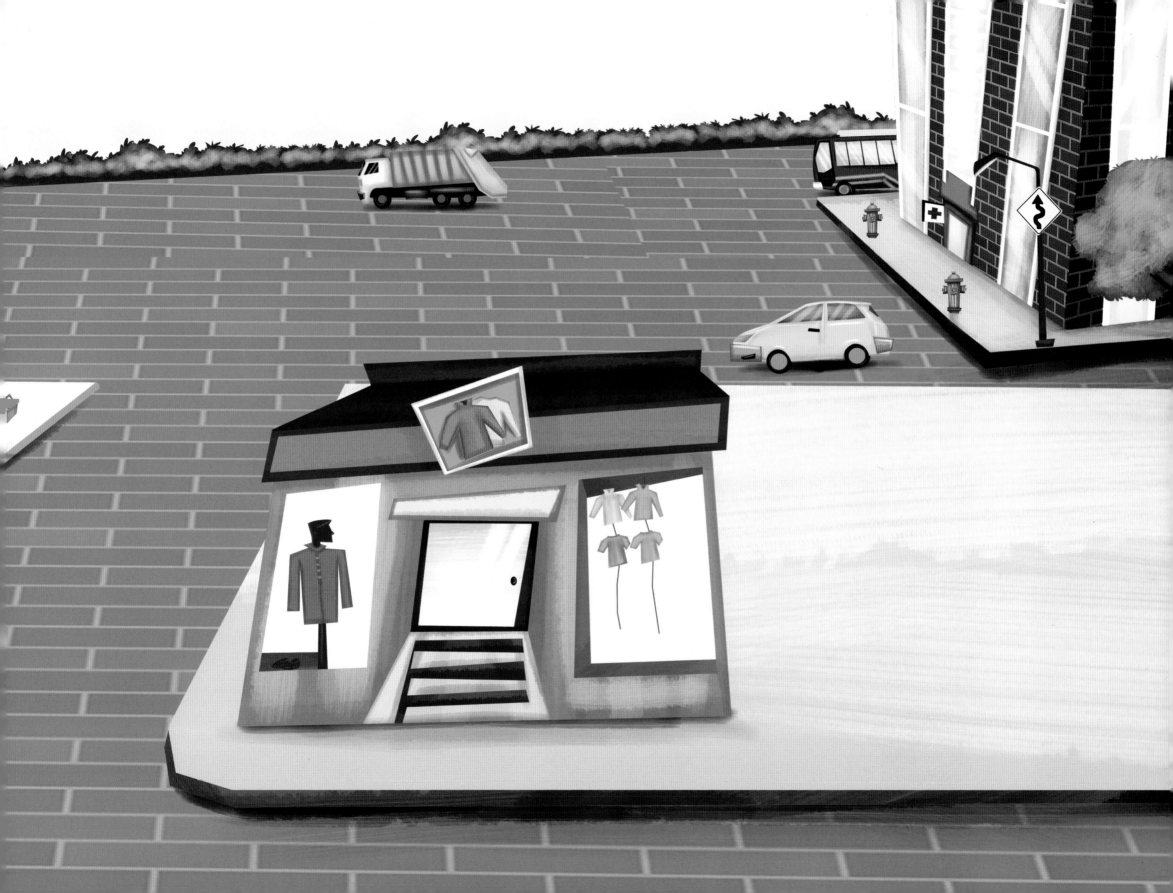

6

7

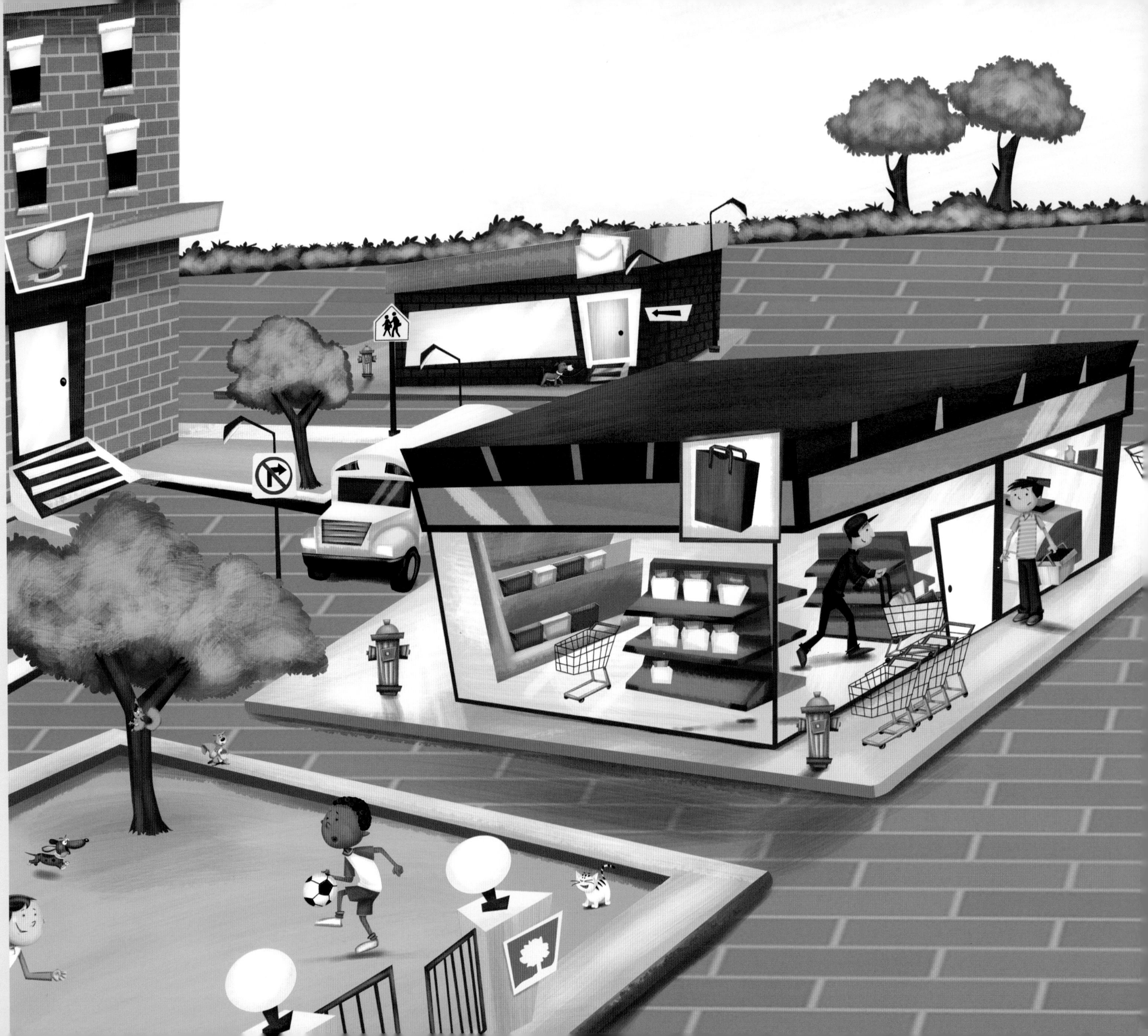

8

9

10